• • • MILAH TOVAH PRESS • • •

HANUKKAH
Activity Book for Kids

A Fun, Festive Book with Coloring Pages, Trivia, Mazes, Games, Puzzles, and More for Jewish Boys and Girls Aged 4-8 to Celebrate the Festival of Lights

 eBookPro Publishing
www.ebook-pro.com

Hanukkah Activity Book for Kids
Milah Tovah Press

Copyright © 2024 Milah Tovah Press
Sudoku puzzles created by puzzlegenerators.com

All rights reserved; No parts of this book may be reproduced or transmitted in any form or by any means, electronic or mechanical, including photocopying, recording, taping, or by any information retrieval system, without the author's explicit permission in writing.

Cover design: Maria Sokhatski

Contact: agency@ebook-pro.com
ISBN 9789655754759

This book belongs to

. . . .

Word Search

Words can be found in any direction (including diagonals) and can overlap each other. Use the word bank below.

```
G  N  I  S  S  E  L  B  H  D
F  A  T  T  L  E  G  A  F  F
L  X  E  O  F  L  L  T  F  F
A  U  G  B  C  L  T  G  V  H
M  K  H  E  E  I  M  I  C  F
E  H  F  L  I  R  H  F  K  A
Z  A  Y  H  M  U  N  T  C  M
F  R  G  W  H  X  Q  S  U  I
M  O  C  H  A  L  L  A  H  L
D  T  M  I  R  A  C  L  E  Y
```

Word Bank

1. gifts
2. gelt
3. flame
4. family
5. torah
6. hallel
7. challah
8. blessing
9. miracle

Dictionary.com

Connect the dots by Numbers

Spot 7 Differences

Copy the picture

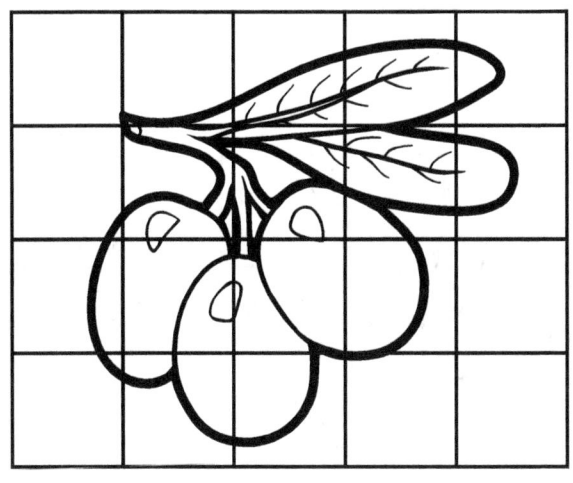

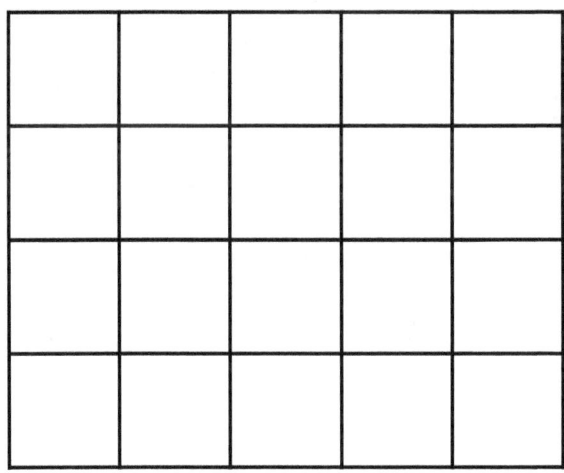

Maze

Color the Picture

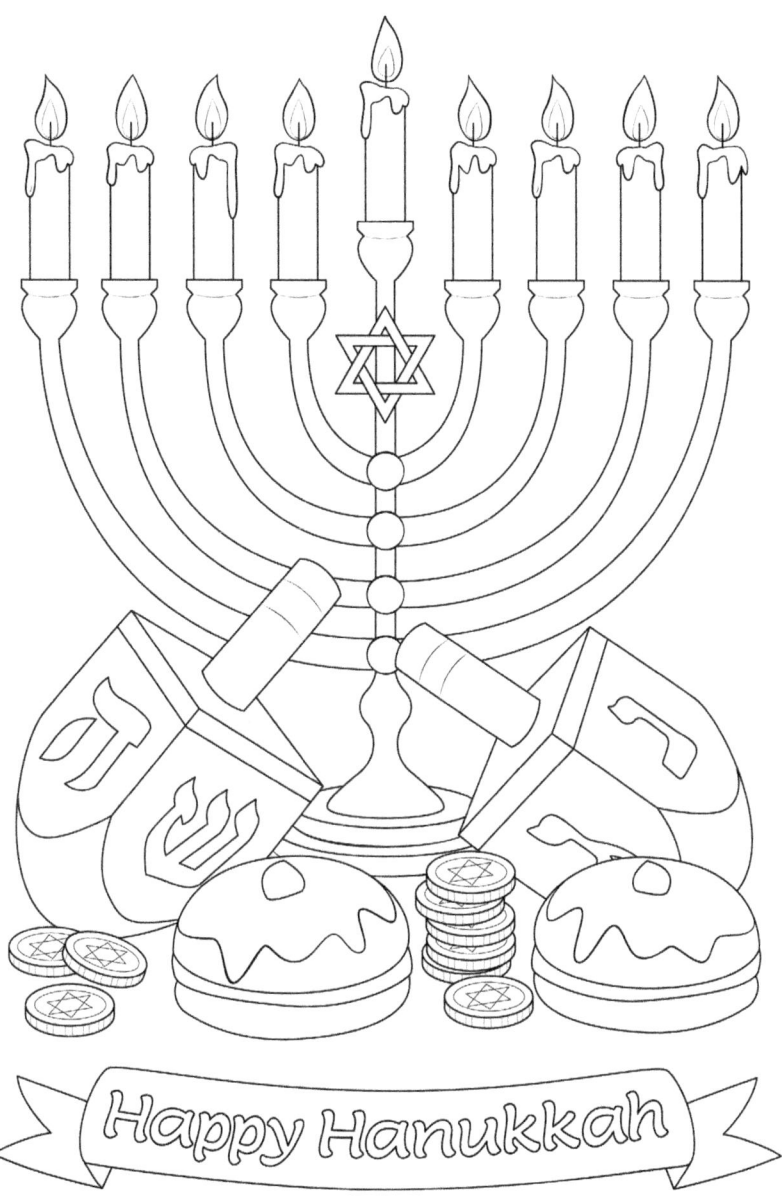

What's a dreidel's favorite kind of music?

...

Rock and roll—because it loves to spin!

Why did the latke refuse to fight the jelly doughnut?

...

It didn't want to get into a sticky situation.

Complete the Picture

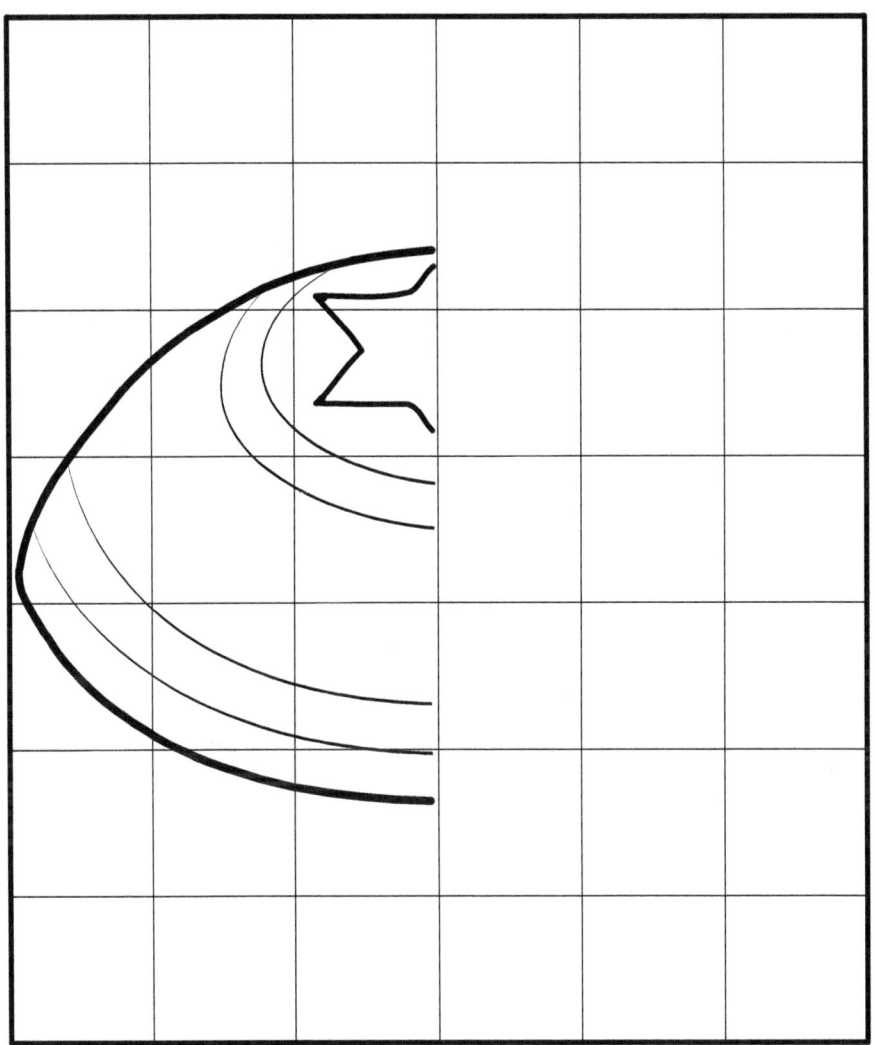

Color the Picture by Numbers

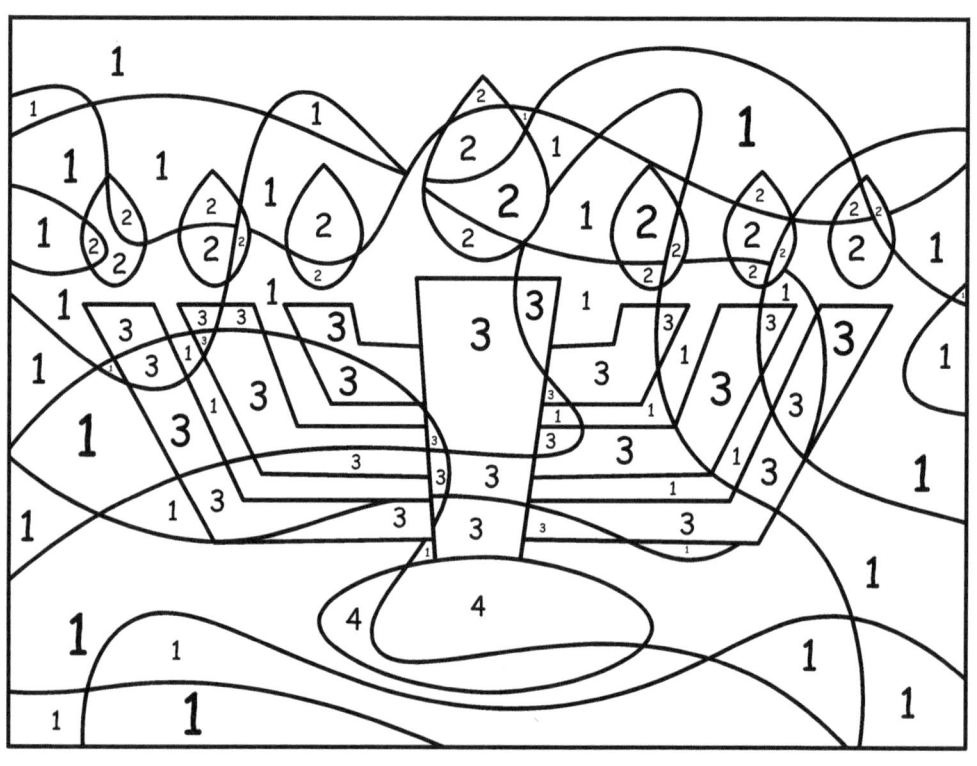

1 violet   2 orange   3 blue   4 green

Unjumble the words

roemnha

....

ledcna

....

voeli loi

....

ledderi

....

kahukanh

....

menorah • candle • olive oil • dreidel • hanukkah

• Draw your own... •

Draw the perfect Hanukkah evening!

Decorate the Menorah

Sudoku

6			7					1
	4				8	3	2	
						7		8
4	2			7	6	8	9	
7	9		4			2	1	3
5	1	8	9					7
8			3	2	9			6
	6				7		3	
3	7	1		6		9	8	

Maze

• Trivia Questions •

Q 1: What is the traditional filling for Hanukkah donuts (sufganiyot)?

Q 2: What is the name of the spinning top traditionally played with on Hanukkah?

Q 3: Why do we celebrate Hanukkah for eight days and eight nights?

Q 4: What is the name of the fried potato pancakes we eat on Hanukkah?

A 1: **Strawberry jelly**

A 2: **Dreidel**

A 3: To commemorate the miracle of the oil that lasted the Maccabees for eight whole days

A 4: **Latkes**

Word Search

Words can be found in any direction (including diagonals) and can overlap each other. Use the word bank below.

```
I  P  R  E  S  E  N  T  S  H
H  A  K  K  U  N  A  H  F  O
K  M  A  C  C  A  B  E  E  L
S  L  Y  T  A  I  S  T  E  I
E  Y  E  P  O  T  N  T  L  D
K  M  R  D  I  C  Z  H  D  A
T  B  C  V  I  Z  J  G  N  Y
A  R  A  I  E  E  K  I  A  L
L  L  O  T  C  Y  R  L  C  V
T  E  M  P  L  E  I  D  J  O
```

Word Bank

1. temple
2. light
3. hanukkah
4. holiday
5. dreidel
6. latkes
7. candle
8. festival
9. maccabee
10. presents

Dictionary.com

• Write your own story •

It was the eighth night of Hanukkah and everyone was in an uproar. The menorah was gone! But who could have taken it? And why?

....
....
....
....
....
....
....
....
....
....
....
....
....
....
....

Color the Picture

Sudoku

6	9			2	4			
	7		3	6		2		
	2		1	7	9			
	5		2	9	6			8
		2		4		7		9
9	8		7	5	1		6	
8						5		4
2	1				5	6	8	
7	4			8			1	3

What do you get when you cross a menorah with a GPS?

...

Lights that tell you exactly where to glow!

What do menorahs do when they're tired?

...

They take a "light" nap!

• Draw your own... •

Draw the moment when the oil lasted for eight days, creating a Hanukkah miracle.

Count the Items

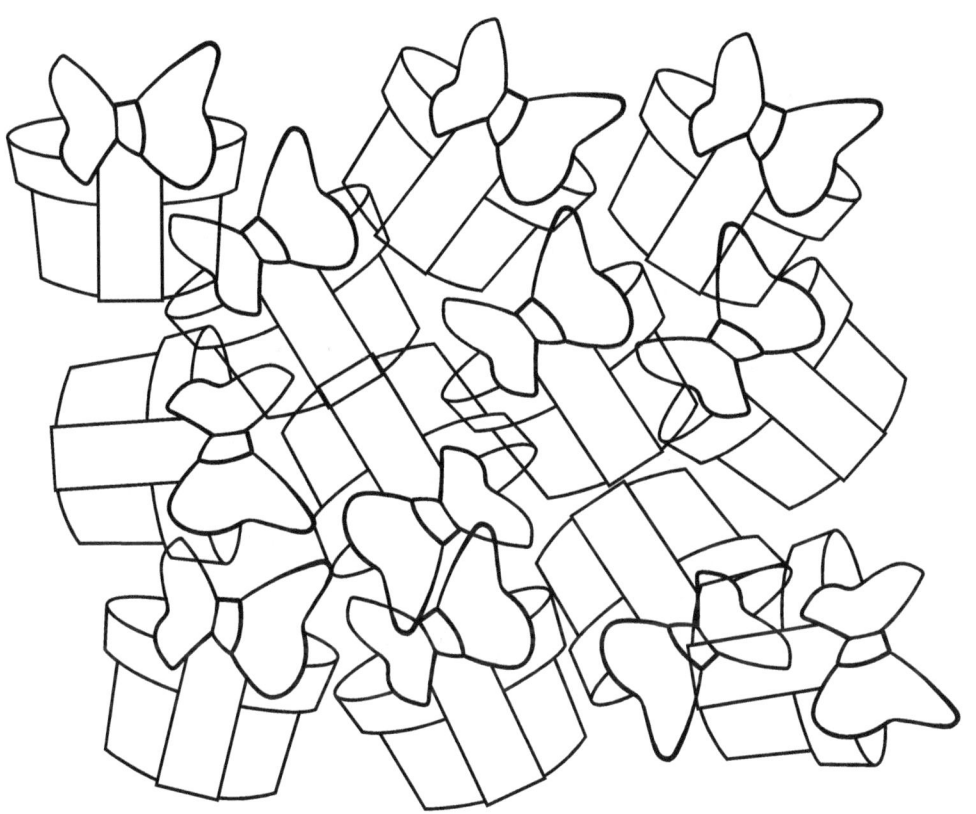

Decorate the Dreidel

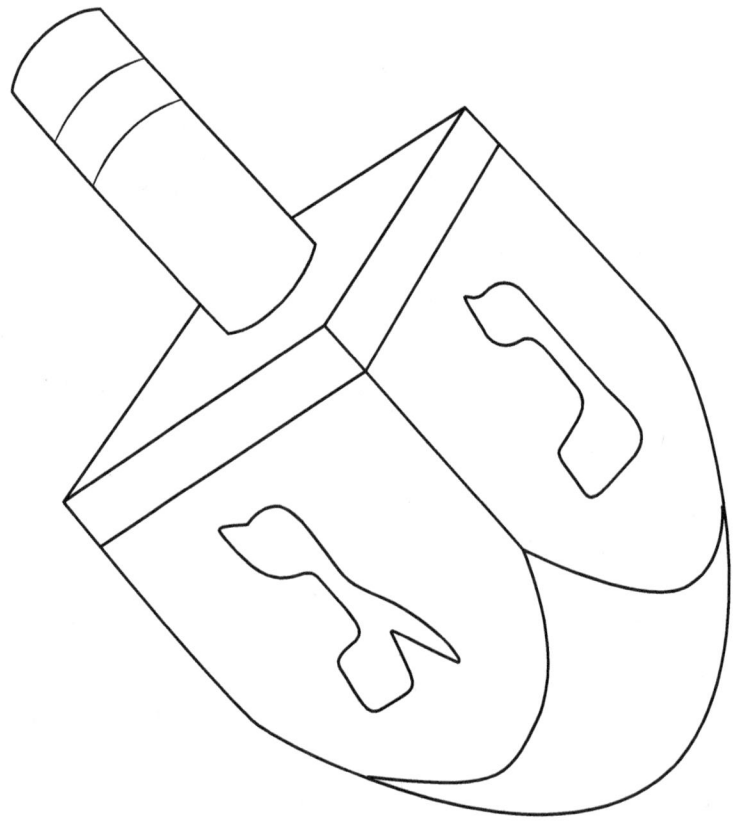

Maze

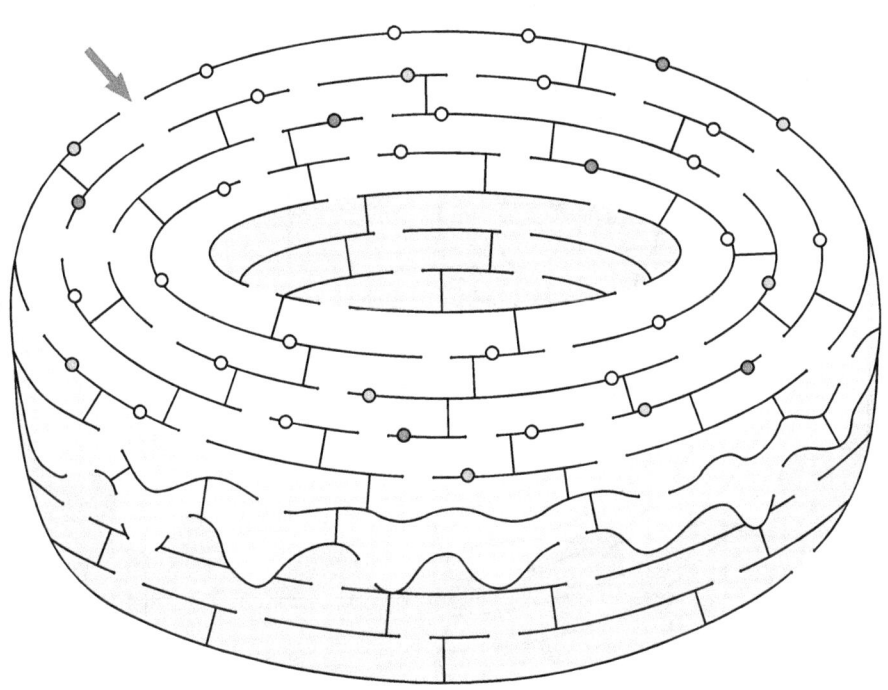

Complete the Picture

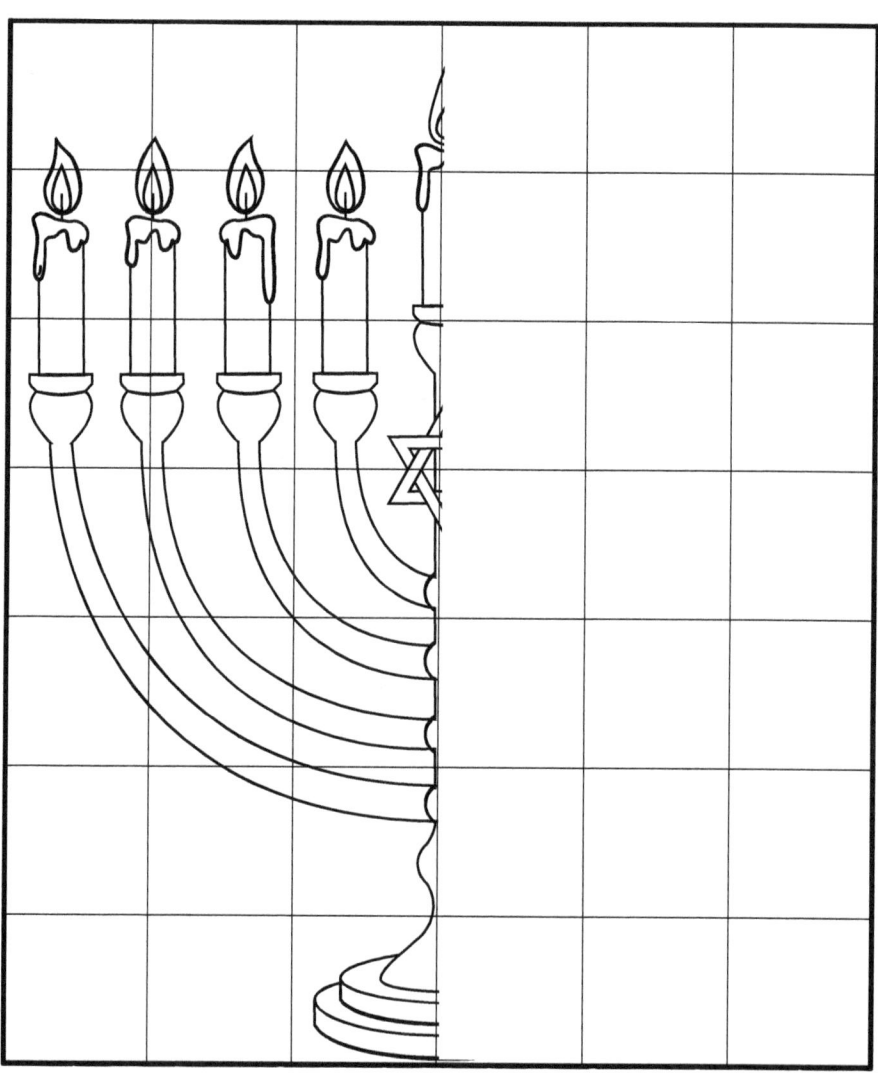

Draw your own...

Draw your favorite Hanukkah foods.

• Trivia Questions •

Q 1: What is Hanukkah Gelt?

Q 2: What is the special name of the ninth candle on the Menorah?

Q 3: What do the letters on the dreidel stand for?

Q 4: How many candles do we light in total over all eight nights of Hanukkah?

A 1: Gifts or money given mainly to children on Hanukkah.

A 2: The Shamash.

A 3: The letters "nun", "gimmel", "heh", and "shin" stand for the Hebrew words: "Nes Gadol Haya Sham" — a great miracle occurred there.

A 4: 44

Sudoku

7	9		6	8		1		
6				2	1	8		
1		8					9	
				7	4	5	2	8
							9	
5				9	8	6	3	7
		5		3	6		8	9
3			8		2	7	4	5
		7	4	5			1	6

Color the Picture

• Draw your own... •

Draw the gifts you'd like to receive for Hanukkah!

Why did the dreidel become a comedian?

...

It loved to spin jokes.

Which hand should you use to light the menorah?

...

Neither, it's best to use a candle.

Write your own story

It was the night before Hanukkah, and Rachel was so excited! She couldn't wait to light the first candle in the Menorah. Rachel fell into a deep sleep, when suddenly...

Complete the Picture

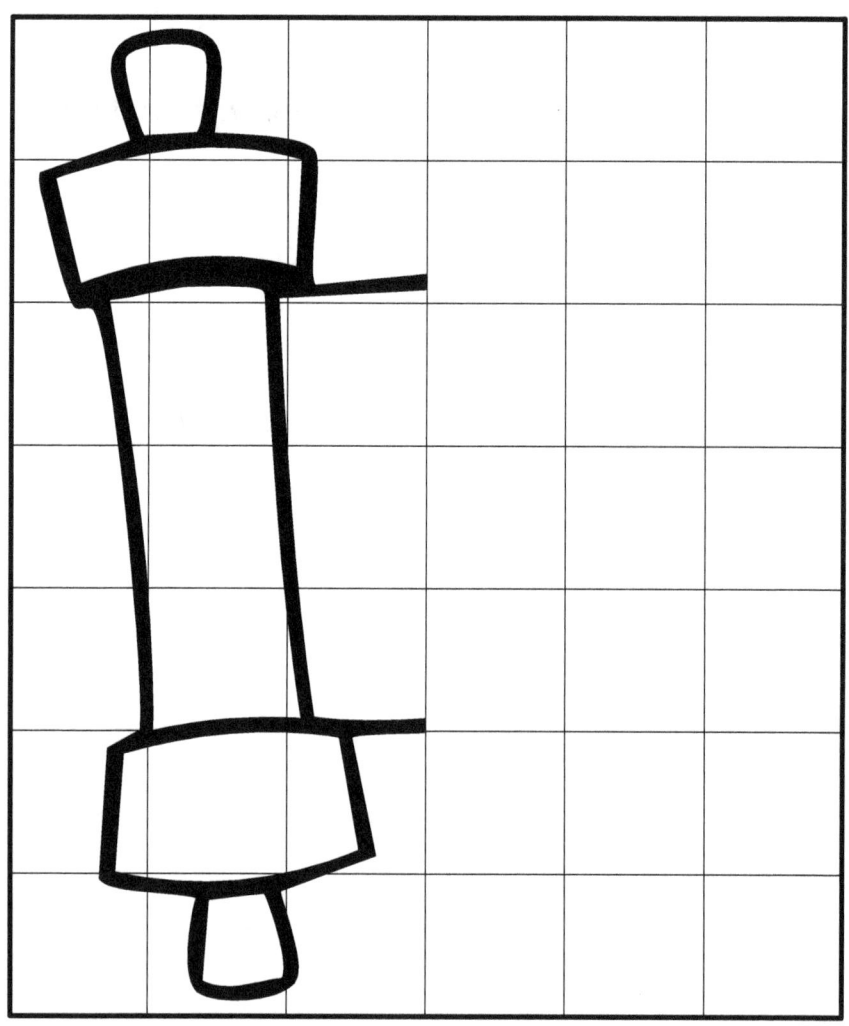

Decorate the Menorah

Maze

Sudoku

1	5			8				2
	8		1		3	4		5
2	6	4	5	9				1
5		7	8		4			
6					5		1	4
					9	2		8
		6			8		2	
9	1			7			4	6
8	3		6		1	5	9	

Unjumble the words

untdo

....

ecbamasec

....

vesikl

....

tiheg

....

tasimrhsc

....

donut • maccabees • kislev • eight • christmas

Color the Picture

Decorate the Dreidel

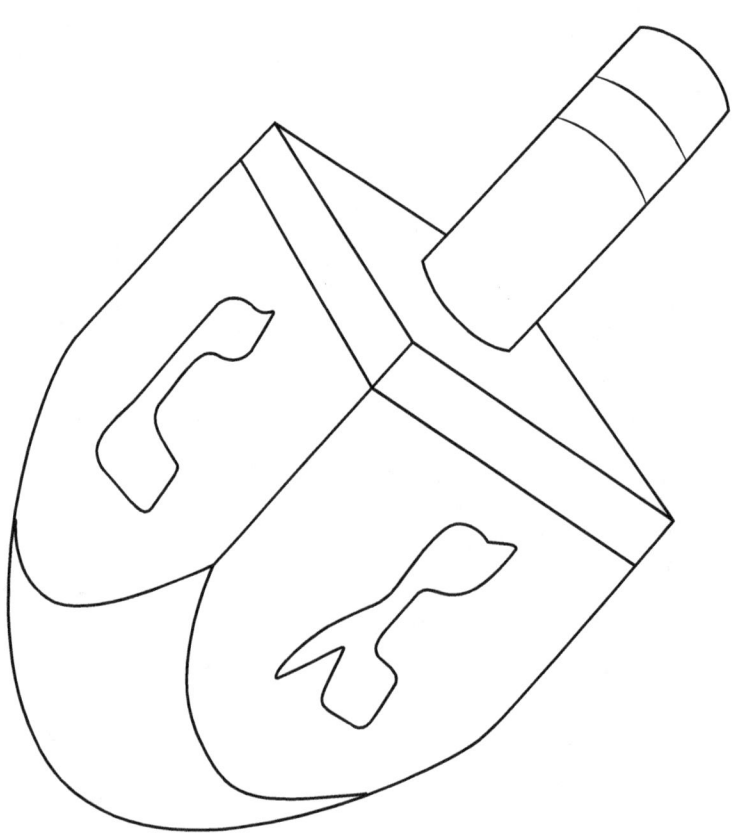

Sudoku

4			6			3		
6		2	7	4	3		9	
	3	8						
5			3	6	9			1
		1	5	2	7			
2	9		8	1		6	5	
9		6	1	7				
	4		9		6	2	1	5
		5		3			6	9

Complete the Picture

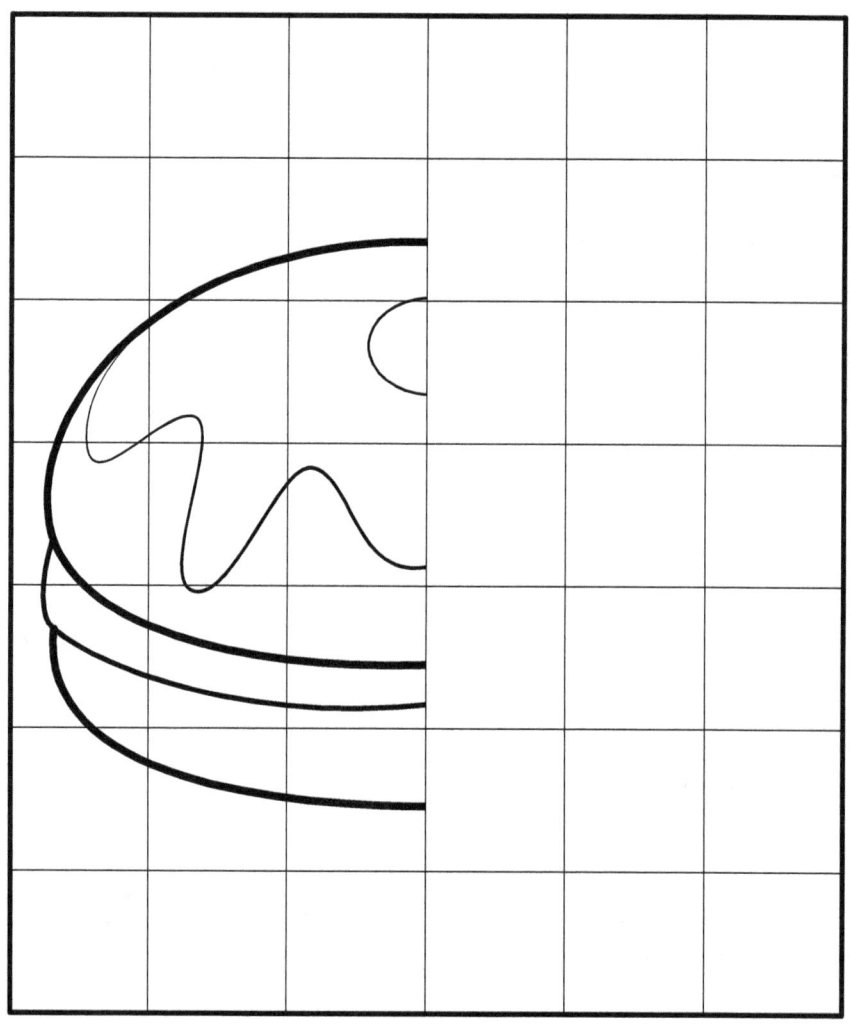

• Trivia Questions •

Q 1: Where do we place the menorah?

Q 2: Why are traditional Hanukkah treats, like latkes and sufganiyot, fried in oil?

Q 3: What are two other major Jewish holidays, besides Hanukkah?

Q 4: How many of Matisyahu's Maccabee sons fought against the Greeks?

A 1: Outside or on a windowsill, for everyone to see and admire.

A 2: In celebration of the miracle of the oil that lasted for eight days and nights.

A 3: Rosh HaShana, Yom Kippur, Sukkot, Purim, Passover, and Shavuot.

A 4: 5.

Write your own story

Haley couldn't decide what to do. She had received invitations for a Hanukkah party and a Christmas party — both on the same day! She thought about it, and came up with a plan.

Word Search

Words can be found in any direction (including diagonals) and can overlap each other. Use the word bank below.

```
G N I S S E L B H D
F A T T L E G A F F
L X E O F L L T F F
A U G B C L T G V H
M K H E E I M I C F
E H F L I R H F K A
Z A Y H M U N T C M
F R G W H X Q S U I
M O C H A L L A H L
D T M I R A C L E Y
```

Word Bank

1. gifts
2. gelt
3. flame
4. family
5. torah
6. hallel
7. challah
8. blessing
9. miracle

• Draw your own... •

Draw how you imagine the Maccabees' battle against the Greeks looked!

Maze

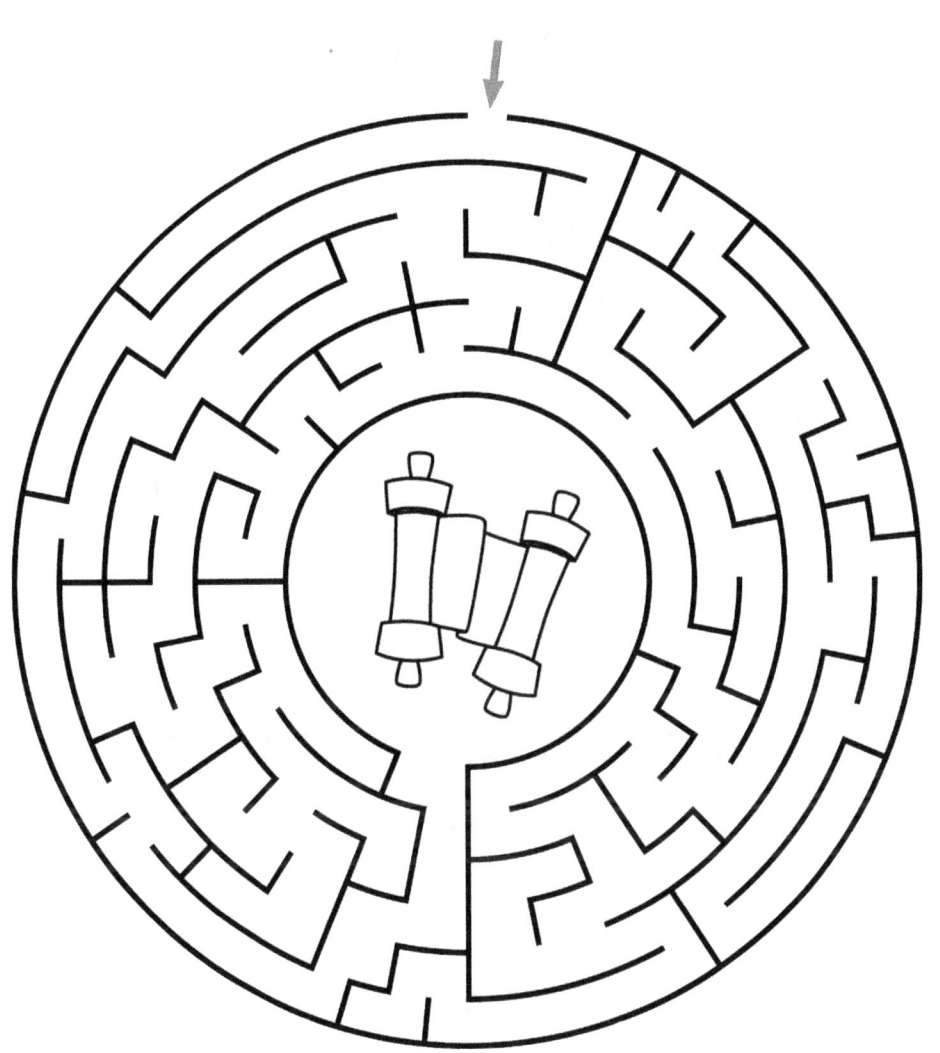

What's the difference between the festival of Hanukkah and a dragon?

...

One is eight nights and the other ate knights.

Why did the donut go to the dentist?

...

To get a filling.

Sudoku

2	6				1	7	9	8	
4		8	2				6		
				4	8		3	2	
5	8	7		6					9
1				9	2				
	2	6	7			4	8		
	4			7	3		1	5	
	7		1	2	5		4		6
	1						7		

Color the Picture

• Write your own story •

Two latkes were sitting in a frying pan. One latke said to the other...

Count the Items

Color the Picture by Numbers

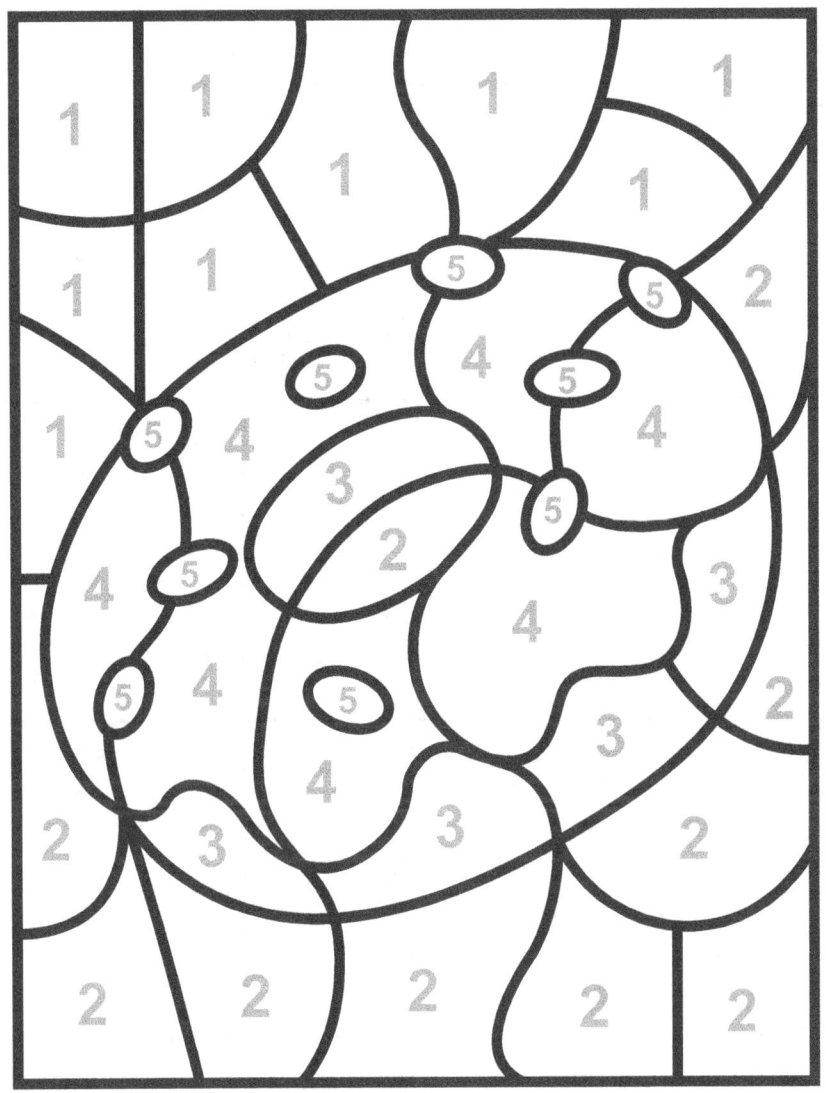

1 light green 2 light green 3 orange 4 pink 5 brown

Sudoku

3	8						9	4
			4		9		3	
4	9			2	5		7	
				6		8	1	5
5		8	9				6	7
		6		5		9	4	
6	5	4	8	9			2	1
8			1	4				
	2	3		7		4		9

Complete the Picture

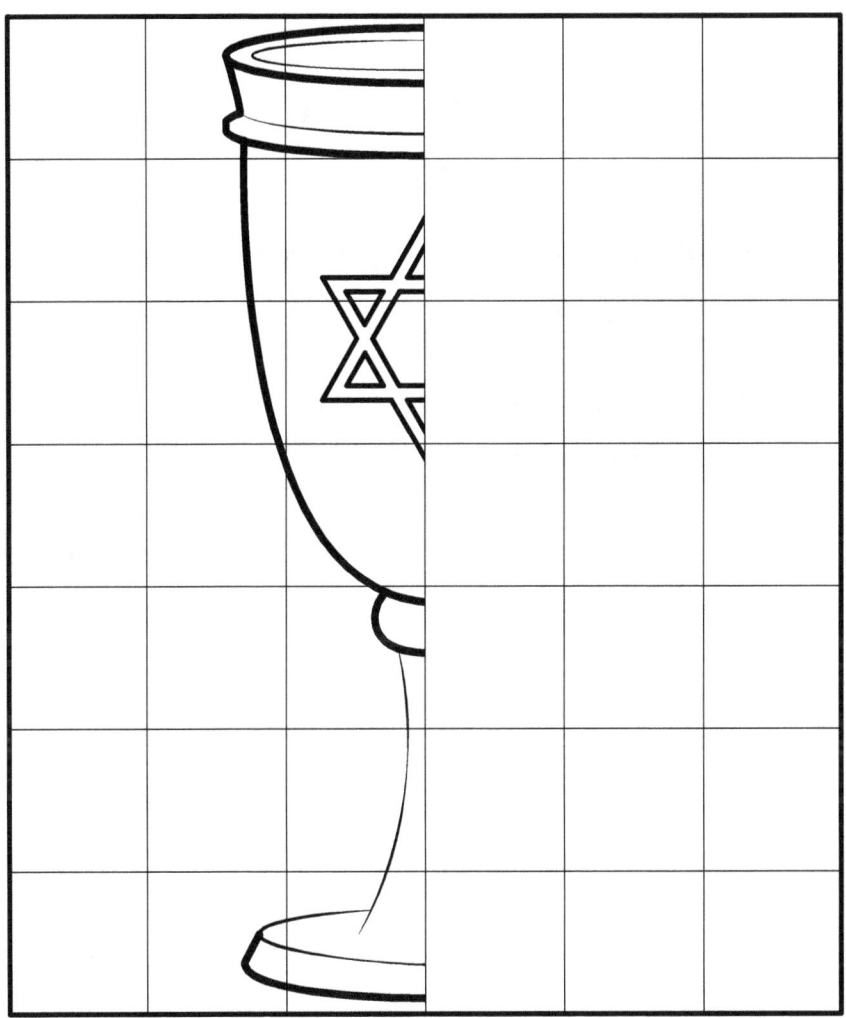

• Trivia Questions •

Q 1: **What is the Yiddish name for sufganiyot: Ponchos, Ponchkes, or Pachniks?**

Q 2: **What did the Maccabees search for in the ruins of the Temple?**

Q 3: **In which Hebrew month do we celebrate the first night of Hanukkah?**

Q 4: **What is the traditional Jewish song sung after lighting the Menorah?**

A 1: Ponchkes.

A 2: Olive oil to light the Menorah with.

A 3: Kislev.

A 4: Maoz Tzur.

• Draw your own… •

Draw the moment when the oil lasted for eight days, creating a Hanukkah miracle.

• Color the Picture •

Sudoku

1	5				9			
4	6		5	1		9		
		9	6	4			1	
					1			
7			9	6	4	2		1
	1	6	7	5				3
6	7	1		2	5	8	3	
		2		9			6	
3			8		6	1	2	4

Unjumble the words

lempte

....

mhashasm

....

ketlas

....

laresjume

....

whijse

....

temple • shammash • latkes • jerusalem • jewish

What did one latke say to the other at the party?

...

"I'm feeling fried, how about you?"

Why do menorahs make great friends?

...

They always light up your life!

Sudoku solutions

P. 16

6	8	2	7	9	3	4	5	1
1	4	7	6	5	8	3	2	9
9	3	5	2	4	1	7	6	8
4	2	3	1	7	6	8	9	5
7	9	6	4	8	5	2	1	3
5	1	8	9	3	2	6	4	7
8	5	4	3	2	9	1	7	6
2	6	9	8	1	7	5	3	4
3	7	1	5	6	4	9	8	2

P. 22

6	9	3	5	2	4	8	7	1
4	7	1	3	6	8	2	9	5
5	2	8	1	7	9	4	3	6
3	5	7	2	9	6	1	4	8
1	6	2	8	4	3	7	5	9
9	8	4	7	5	1	3	6	2
8	3	6	9	1	7	5	2	4
2	1	9	4	3	5	6	8	7
7	4	5	6	8	2	9	1	3

P. 31

7	9	4	6	8	3	1	5	2
6	5	3	9	2	1	8	7	4
1	2	8	5	4	7	9	6	3
9	3	6	1	7	4	5	2	8
8	7	2	3	6	5	4	9	1
5	4	1	2	9	8	6	3	7
4	1	5	7	3	6	2	8	9
3	6	9	8	1	2	7	4	5
2	8	7	4	5	9	3	1	6

P. 39

1	5	3	4	8	6	9	7	2
7	8	9	1	2	3	4	6	5
2	6	4	5	9	7	3	8	1
5	2	7	8	1	4	6	3	9
6	9	8	2	3	5	7	1	4
3	4	1	7	6	9	2	5	8
4	7	6	9	5	8	1	2	3
9	1	5	3	7	2	8	4	6
8	3	2	6	4	1	5	9	7

P. 43

4	1	9	6	5	8	3	7	2
6	5	2	7	4	3	1	9	8
7	3	8	2	9	1	5	4	6
5	7	4	3	6	9	8	2	1
8	6	1	5	2	7	9	3	4
2	9	3	8	1	4	6	5	7
9	2	6	1	7	5	4	8	3
3	4	7	9	8	6	2	1	5
1	8	5	4	3	2	7	6	9

P. 51

2	6	3	5	1	7	9	8	4
4	5	8	2	3	9	6	7	1
7	9	1	6	4	8	3	2	5
5	8	7	3	6	1	2	4	9
1	3	4	8	9	2	5	6	7
9	2	6	7	5	4	8	1	3
6	4	2	9	7	3	1	5	8
8	7	9	1	2	5	4	3	6
3	1	5	4	8	6	7	9	2

P. 56

3	8	2	6	1	7	5	9	4
7	6	5	4	8	9	1	3	2
4	9	1	3	2	5	6	7	8
9	3	7	2	6	4	8	1	5
5	4	8	9	3	1	2	6	7
2	1	6	7	5	8	9	4	3
6	5	4	8	9	3	7	2	1
8	7	9	1	4	2	3	5	6
1	2	3	5	7	6	4	8	9

P. 61

1	5	7	2	3	9	6	4	8
4	6	3	5	1	8	9	7	2
2	8	9	6	4	7	3	1	5
5	2	4	3	8	1	7	9	6
7	3	8	9	6	4	2	5	1
9	1	6	7	5	2	4	8	3
6	7	1	4	2	5	8	3	9
8	4	2	1	9	3	5	6	7
3	9	5	8	7	6	1	2	4

www.ingramcontent.com/pod-product-compliance
Lightning Source LLC
LaVergne TN
LVHW020430070526
838199LV00004B/340